We The People,
Not We The Government

We The People, Not We The Government

✦

WAKE UP AMERICA

MA'XIMO

iUniverse, Inc.
New York   Bloomington

We The People, Not We The Government

WAKE UP AMERICA

iUniverse books may be ordered through booksellers or by contacting:

iUniverse
1663 Liberty Drive
Bloomington, IN 47403
www.iuniverse.com
1-800-Authors (1-800-288-4677)

ISBN: 978-1-4401-0360-5 (pbk)
ISBN: 978-1-4401-0361-2 (ebk)

Printed in the United States of America

WE THE PEOPLE
WAKE UP
AMERICA!

Introduction

This book is relating to some of our past, what our nation was truly about, the morals, integrity, pride for our flag, and what it means to be an American. What are we doing to our country? What type of future are we leaving for our children and their children? Will they be able to look back, and see that what was beautiful is still beautiful and respected? The Constitution is written on Godly Laws and Biblical principals.

We need to remind ourselves that when we were children we all played with our imaginary friends. We had games such as hop scotch, marbles, jump rope, jacks, and yoyo. The boys would like to be police officer, doctor, firefighters, G.I. Joe, cowboy, and racecar driver. These were hopes and dreams that we had. If our families were to ask what do you want to be when you grow up? You may answer a singer, dancer, a teacher, or clown in the circus. Something that only our inner most desire made us feel good all over when we expressed it. Our role models were our parents, brother, or sister. If you chose someone outside of the family, they might be the same person our parents admired.

To become a professional you had to get trained, educated, certified and sometimes licensed to qualify. We do not regard any one who claims to be a professional without education, experience or certification. We are compromising to more understand what is wrong than what is right under God. There are those who want us to look the other way, so whenever some one is wrong we justify it to excuse the wrong.. We should STOP using the expression politically correct. If we were voting on anything, it was always the majority over the minority. We are allowing one or two to decide what the mass of the people should be doing or how we should live. Looking back at the nineteenth century, children respected adults and their elders. The children of today have no trepidation of authority.

I am of Spanish descendent born in Colon the Republic of Panama, brought here by my Father in 1957 not knowing where I was going only understanding that I was to meet my mother after arriving. My sister and I saw for the first time the Statue of Liberty through a port-hole of a ship. My Dad then explained to us that we were in New York Harbor in the United States.

I was too young to have any special feeling on what was different from my home than being in the United States. I have never returned to my home country I have claimed here to be my country. Every American should listen to the National Anthem and gaze upon the Flag. It is something to experience. Observe the expression of an Olympic Athlete's face while they are receiving their Gold, Silver or Bronze medals.

So many men and women have given more than just time to this country. They have sacrificed blood sweat and separation from their families.

Sacrificing their personal ambition and putting their careers on hold. We habitually take it for granted…then there are those who can't stand the fact that we have it so easy. The sick ones (high school or college student and terrorist) remind us it can all be taken away by those who live in our own country and claim to be Americans. That was proven with Columbine, D.C. Sniper and the 911 attack. Some believe that our President and FBI were aware and nothing was done.

We are ready for change and fresh youthful ideals and ideas so our children and grandchildren may have what we have taken for granted.

Our Fighting Soldiers
Our Heroes
Wake Up America!

Parallel to self and so many others who have served in WWI & II, Korean, Viet-Nam, Gulf, Dessert Storm, and Iraq Veterans have sacrificed for the future of this country and protection of our families. Family that is left may even have questions regarding the death of a loved one. The truth must be told, for instance Cpl. Pat Tillman was killed by a Ranger in his own unit on April 22nd 2004 in Afghanistan when his unit was hastily split up in hostile territory just before sunset. The Army medical examiner found three closely grouped bullets holes in Cpl. Tillman's head. He was cut down by a Ranger with a M16 rifle from a mere 10 yards away. The Pentagon tried to cover up the truth by presenting The Silver Star to the Tillman's Family (White, 2005). They deserve the *TRUTH.*

Another cover up; three years ago on July 19, 2005, army Private First Class LaVena Johnson was found dead in Balad, Iraq. Her body was found in a tent belonging to the private military contractor KBR. She had abrasions all over her body, a broken nose, a black eye, burned hands, loose teeth, acid burns on her genitals and a bullet in her head. The Army labeled Johnson's death a suicide. Her parents never believed that story, they believe she was raped and murder and are demanding a full congressional investigation (Democracy Now, 2008).

As a Marine escort I know that the military have sent love ones home to families under false depiction of death. I was stationed at Marine Barracks Portsmouth, Va., while encountering these occurrences to cover up incompetence and public humiliation of having to pay serious law suit for those who died under government care. Military personnel are compelled to secrecy calling it national security. Military soldiers have died at the hands of the Government they trust.

As a Marine not yet married. I joined the U.S. Marine Corps on December 1968 so I could secure a way of life for my immigrant family and myself to become citizens. I served twenty-one years and woke up late in my military career realizing that we were mistreated, and disrespected through out my entire service.

The same government who employed me taxed me. We the American fighting men and women are tax for what we do while on active and reserve service. What type of Government or should I say Businessmen and politicians are running this country? The veterans, who survived the war and made it to retirement, have to battle again to receive proper medical treatment. You are expected to give your health insurance information, so [they] Veterans

Administration can save money that Congress has already allocated for our benefit.

This allows the Head of the Veterans Administration [idiot] to say that he is staying within budget to save the Government money. He gets a raise and the veterans receive poor medical care. Our job is done we are no longer needed throw them out with the wash water is what I perceive this to be. The care we receive is not of concern but of regard that [they] nurses and doctors "not all" are doing us a favor to assist us. There are large retirement cities where [they] are so under-staffed and unequipped to handle the large number of vets requiring care. Really, they did not expect us to live as long as we have.

Emergencies are seen at the end of all scheduled appointments. Appointments are schedule for three to six months in order to be seen by a doctor. Don't let it be that you are late by ten or fifteen minutes, you will be reschedule for the next early availability which is in three or four months. There are some cases where a veteran has travel for as little as one hour or as far as three hours. They're means to travel to clinic would be to take a shuttle that would only pick at certain time even if their appointment is later in the day, must sit around all day till the last patient is seen for a shuttle ride back or get a member of the family to take off work to provide transportation for you. The large dose of drugs is not safe to drive for the possibility of sleeping behind the wheel or having a stroke. I was faced with that numerous times.

As a young 19 year old U.S. Marine returning from Viet Nam in the winter of November 1970 under the Nixon Administration.

My separation was conducted at Camp Pendleton California. The separation staff did not debrief those returning from Viet Nam. We were not informed of experiencing any flash backs of physical combat or nervousness heavy sweating while sleeping, or that we could seek assistance at a V.A. Clinic. While walking among citizens and if there is back fire of an automobile don't hit the [deck] ground and roll for cover. People will look at you as if you are weird or crazy. No one told us that we would want to sleep with a pistol or sleep on the [deck] floor to feel comfortable. No one told us that we would experience flashbacks of war in our heads and sleep causing us to automatically react to military training that was drilled in our memory. No one ever told us we would still hear the screams and see bodies blown to pieces long after we were released from the military. No one told us!

Upon returning home after two years of servicing as a Marine, I lived with my mother and three younger sisters. It was difficult sleeping at night. I could not get the images out of my head. The outburst scared my siblings and mother they were afraid to approach me. Mom would yell at me and tell me she did not know what they did to me, but I was not the same as before. I recall when she embraced me one day while crying and said, what did they do to my son?

Oh! I was told what to expect while I was a private in boot camp. I was told how to keep alert for the Viet Cong, how to shoot a rifle, pistol and be an expert in doing so. How to ready for Gas or Chemical attack the importance that you only have seconds to protect your self and your fellow marine. I found myself after returning home, how singing military chants whenever I felt cornered or threatened especially when I would board a subway or city bus. Oh! Did I get the stare, and people moving away. I would approach the bullies who picked on me to challenge them to be stupid. I was not able to keep a job because I saw most men around me as weak dirt bag cowards.

My primary job was to be a trained infantry "killer" with leadership ability and common sense. My first enlistment was for two years. I was not offered Project Transition because I only served for two years. These vocational schools were to help those who needed to continue an adjustment for civilian society. It was a service offered to men or women who served four years or more if you didn't come in under a technical field. You were given the opportunity to seek a civilian job where you actually attend their place of business and work for six months and receive a salary with the Marines until you were discharged. I knew that if I stayed home I would have to kill some one. I went back to my original recruiter and reenlisted for four years. Little did I know, what I was experiencing [PTSD] Post Traumatic Stress Disorder. Once I rejoined I felt rejoined to my Band of Brother which is a unique society.

The Regan Administration cut the Project Transition to cut the Budget and Survivor Benefit.

I later married my High School sweet heart and had two beautiful daughters. They suffered the awful badgering of my sickness for the first five years until she feared for my daughters being so afraid of their daddy. I would go in and out of emotional episodes. My wife abandoned me, while I was performing my duties as a Drill Instructor shaping future Marines.

Later she filed for a divorce leaving my girls without a Dad. Ten years later she passed a way at the young age of forty five. Leaving my daughter's in the hands of their Grand-parents, still fearing their Dad.

I married a 2nd time and she also experienced the same fears mainly at night but divorced me after ten years. I consider her dead for how she was unreliable and kept my name. She is the Diablo. My immediate family do not communicated with me to this day. My 3rd wife a soul sent from God has been able to understand me and bridge the gap with my family. It's been thirty some years that I am now reuniting with some of my family.

The Disable American Veteran case holder would always tell the veteran that he/she has to submit a letter requesting approval for his/her case to be heard by the board for a rating increase. These board members are usually none military people. I know for a fact I have sat before a board twice in 14 years. Each time I would ask each member if they served in active duty their response was no. They would ultimately make a decision of 10% to 100% if you proved your case. I now believe that U.S. would rather our fighting men and women to die than reward the medals or disability benefits. These board members would ask for the veteran to bring military and medical records to substantiate their claim that's being brought before them. If the record does not show any of the military claims while in service the claim was rejected whether there was a complaint or injury. As a Marine, Special Forces, Ranger or Green Bret, we were not entrusted with any of our Medical records. So for the twenty one years I served in the Marine Corps. Whenever orders were given it was for a pistol, rifle and, sea bags to take to our next command. So how were we able to have specific information on all our medical entry and x-rays that would prove a claim?

The Commanding Officers in charge know the rules, because they were the ones that enforced them. We were told all you need to do is request them whenever you need them. Orders were sent to the individual male or female marine or soldier from Washington, D.C. and your job was to receive and except them to include either two weeks leave or thirty days leave depending on the length of your tour or how much leave you had remaining for the end of that fiscal year. You are not given the liberty to refuse those orders unless under special circumstances.

It has been my experience that if I were a frequent smoker, drinker of booze, drug induce individual I would not survive 18 years of my retirement.

Most of my colleagues past away because of the induce barrage of medications that the practicing physicians and psychologist would just have you to believe taking drugs would help.

Doctors were taken a survey or guessing at what works. Doctors were only treating you according to written guidelines on how to keep the veteran confused and with no hope of cure.

As it is in my case: being prescribed CITALOPRAM HYDROBROMIDE 40MG at bedtime for mood, VALPROVIC ACID 250MG also for mood, or if needed lets try SERTRALINE HCL 100MG you need to take it for the first six days at bedtime and then half for another six days.

It would affect my normal sex drive.

Imagine mothers your sons not able to give you the grand-children you look forward too or wives your love one not able to perform their husbandly duties. DIAZEPAM 10 MG also at night for anxiety which can make you drowsy and not safe to drive alert. Let's not forget that if you also encounter knee, joints and back injury by jump training from planes as most of us have, because of the years of grueling work or constant hours of being around loud jet-engines aircraft-carriers, being aboard submarines. ETODOLAC 300 MG for pain and inflammation. These are all Post Traumatic Stress Disorder or [PTSD]. Our young men and women have suffered at war protecting this country. We are looked upon as another body that made it back let's do little or nothing for them. The Veterans Medical Administration still maintain these practices. Another false hope is to have us meet in group counseling to hash out what we are experiencing so they can say it's on the books that we are supporting these veterans. The best way to support us is either get us quality jobs or pay us our disability. Visit any local Veterans Clinic or Hospital and you will see scores of retired or newly discharged veterans are just waiting like lambs to slaughter. This is the thanks that our Congresspersons and Senators who never served in the military perceive that they are serving their country. Let's not confuse serving in the "Government" as a politician is the same as serving in the military sacrificing your life with minimal pay and poor healthcare. Government officials are serving themselves to a bigger pay check and guess who's footing the bill? **We the people!**

Most of us have anxiety attacks when we have to visit the V.A. Hospital. I have always had my blood pressure jump so high that my reason for such action is I have had doctors wanting to operate. They pack the waiting rooms with so many patients waiting for hours, and only being seen for ten or fifteen minutes. We're asked, how are you? Without thought we always say fine or if not you say awful they ask, what's your pain level from one to ten, all general questions as if they don't have your records in front of them. Their job is to frustrate you and piss you off. Every medication they prescribe they charge us. The men and women, sons and daughters who gave their life for this country's continue freedom. We are the same men and women who volunteered to join the service. Again our congress person should serve at least eight years in the military and not all in the states. They need to experience separation from their family. After experiencing those hardships can they truly understand what the military personnel go through?

The Director of Veterans Administration has said that he has adequate funds to maintain the disable, paraplegics, handicap, and PTSD. The current Bush Administration is looking to cut back financial funding for veterans. There are Senators who are not supporting any of the continuation of retirement pension and medical aid for all active and reserve Guard. These Senators are from Arizona men and women who have never served in the military that are supporting these issues. We have become so complacent to what our representatives say that we do not question anything. Each one of us, have the ability to do something about it. Let us stop saying, I am only one person. We need to form a link join together and take back our country our AMERICA we can do it! We need to get angry and make sacrifices. What do we know that makes people realize that you are serious? When you cripple their livelihood or mess with their money. We have to realize that we can not just elect people who are not natural born to give them the impression that they are eligible for election to highest office in the nation.

We should not amend the Constitution no matter how popular the individual. That's one sure way for us to allow someone who walks like a duck, but is not really looking out for the best of America. These and all public officials who are not American born, should at least serve in the U.S. Forces so their background check can be scrutinize and should be made to serve for more than two or four years. The requirement should be eight years.

Senator Obama I recommend you should consider these names; for a running mate Ret. General Colin Powel or Ms. Condoleezza Rice and they will put aside their personal feelings to accomplish the job that needs to be done. This is based on their qualifications and expertise and not what the members of Congress think. This is not a Game Show.

Our Nation is at the turning point of the millennium we must continue to give of ourselves unselfishly for the future of our children and our freedom. Let us all come together now, be a strong link and pull together. Be a leader in our own house and not try and change other countries, let them grow and follow our leadership. They will get the idea just by our example. We must be good stewards and then they will ask for our help or guidance. I plan to be around for my grandchildren to grow up and their children to grow up. Own a Sky-car to see them when-ever I so desire. This is a Wake Up for a Marine Veteran and an American.

Our Government Officials
Wake Up America!

We the people are electing city officials Mayors, Governor's, Congresspersons, Senators, Presidents, Supreme Courts Justices are being appointed, and their credentials are to tell us the great bull to society and giving us what they think we want to hear. It is not to say that these individual's did not have an education, such as a law degree or business degree. Politicians think that since they know how to run a business they can run the nation's business as their own, and that is where we fail. These facts are found on CRS Report for Congress under: www.usgovinfo.com ,

The Sunday Show Meet the Press… with Tom Brokaw he met with particular Governor Arnold Schwarzenegger is mentioned that he has not yet decided to support Senator McCain. Tom asked what are your feeling about the Presidency he said his good friends the Bush have promise to work something out with the Constitution to find a loop hole.

Here is a man born in Austria his father Gustav Schwarzenegger volunteered to join the Austrian Nazi party when it was still illegal to do in 1938.

Did you know!

Gustav later became the Police Chief in the town of Thal bei Graz where Arnold grew up. The media has skillfully focused on his father and away from all the real Nazi connections and said, "Arnold isn't responsible for what his daddy did."

What we do not hear is that Arnold is a self-proclaimed follower of Kurt Waldheim. Kurt was a favorite of the United Nations and served as Secretary General from 1972 to 1982.

When Kurt Waldheim ran for the Presidency of Austria in 1986, Arnold was Waldheim's biggest supporter and campaigned across Austria. He was featured on campaign posters.

Let us think about this!

Don't be fooled by the dog and pony show know as the California recall-it's filled with extremely high levels of illuminati and Schwarzenegger's Nazi and New World Order Links.

Most Americans think as I do that Arnold Schwarzenegger as a charismatic bodybuilder who became a famous Hollywood actor,

Married into the Kennedy clan. Beneath the façade of Arnold's joking [untruth] an intricate web of evil including Nazi war criminals, occult rituals, a friendship with one head of the UN and known Nazi, Kurt Waldheim, Warren Buffett {the oracle of Omaha} and many others.

On one level, the California recall election is a giant diversion, providing a smoke screen that obscures hundreds of pertinent developments in our world every day. The media circus feeding frenzy plays their part in over dramatization.

At the same time, the California recall of 2003, when examined from a larger perspective, reveals many of the dark workings inside the New World Order. It is important to note that even if Gary Davis stays in office or if Cruz Bustamante is elected the result will remain the same.

Whether they are Republican or Democrat, all of the candidates being given serious media attention, are anti gun, pro abortion, and promoters of big centralized government.

The giant Recall sideshow serves the elite by creating the illusion that California's problems have been caused by bad fiscal policy alone.

In reality, California is an admitted beta testing model for elite social engineers. The head of the Simon Wiesenthal Center, Rabbi Marvin Hier has defended Schwarzenegger saying that Arnold had no connection to Nazis.

Of course the fact that Arnold has tithed a percentage of every film he has starred in {reportedly over five(5) million dollars} in the last eighteen years to the Simon Wiesenthal Center does a lot to explain why the Simon

Wiesenthal Center gave him their highest award (The National Leadership Award) in 1997.

Did you know our Arnold!

The whole world learned that the United Nations had known all along that Kurt Waldheim was a Nazi and a wanted war criminal and helped cover it up. The Waldheim story that broke in 1986 was a sensation and dominated news cycles for months.

Arnold Schwarzenegger, stood up at his wedding and with Maria Shriver in front of a crowd of east coast blue bloods and said, " My friends don't want me to mention Kurt's name because of all the recent Nazi stuff and the UN controversy, but I love him and Marie does too, and so thank you, Kurt.

When Arnold's father died, his mother married the Head of the Austrian Parliament, who himself was a Colonel in the SS. While filming the documentary "Pumping Iron", Arnold told reporters he admired Adolf Hitler and other dictators.

While the Simon Wiesenthal Center is defending Arnold, they are busy waging a smear campaign against Mel Gibson for producing a biblically accurate reenactment of the last day of Christ's life, in his new movie, The Passion.

The ADL and the Simon Wiesenthal Center have demanded Gibson re-edit the film, threatening to boycott its release and are claiming that the film has already generated hatred, despite the fact that only a few thousand people have seen it in private screenings.

A month before Schwarzenegger announced that he was throwing his hat into the ring; most of the national media was reporting that Arnold was not going to run.

Infowars.com came across an article in the July 23, 2003 San Francisco Chronicle that contracted the prevailing view of the political gurus.

The article reported, "The Republican hierarchy would favor Schwarzenegger. At least that's the word that came out of the Bohemian Grove that past weekend, where a number of state and national GOPers, including presidential adviser Karl Rove, happened to be gathered at a club getaway."

Of course, the Bohemian Club favors Arnold: he married into an illuminati bloodline in 1986, and soon after became a member of the Grove.

[The Bohemian Grove is and elite encampment founded in 1872. Presidents have been attending the yearly fifteen-day meeting since 1901]

In 2000 [two weeks before the official announcement was made] CNN reported that Dick Cheney was to be George W. Bush's running mate. CNN said that they had garnered the information from network executives present at the Bohemian Grove's encampment where they learned of the choice of Cheney from George Hubert Walker Bush and Collin Powell.

This is not the first time big political decision to be made by a select few at this all-male elite gathering. According to annuals published by Bohemian Club, the Star Wars program was hatched there in 1978 and the Manhattan Project were conceived at the Grove.

Economist Alan Greenspan made his first visit to the Bohemian Grove in 1984 before it is announced that he was being appointed Chairman of the Federal Reserve.

The Washington Times, Spy magazine, and many other prestigious publications have reported on the homosexual orgies and bizarre rituals that take place at the Grove. Respected papers have documented the migration of high dollar male and female prostitutes from Europe and America yearly to the nearby town of Monte Rio, which serves as a watering hole for the members of the all-male Bohemian Club [a club made up of our so-called Christian conservative leaders].

Schwarzenegger's connections do not stop at the Grove. An article published by Reuters, titled "Buffett's back with the Terminator," described Arnold and Warren Buffett descending by helicopter to a meeting at the ancestral home of the Rothschild Dynasty.

The article stated that, "Among those invited to Waddesdon manor were like of James Wolfensohn

President of the World Bank, Jorma Ollila, chief executive of Nokia and De Beers chairman Nicky

Oppenheimer" [head of the world diamond monopoly]. The story continued to describe how the illuminati "chieftain" greeted Arnold. "A group of photographers captured the moment when Buffett and Schwarzenegger, resplendent in steel-tipped cowboy boots, stepped onto Waddesdon's freshly cut lawn to be greeted by Lord Jacob Rothchild.

"It's very nice of you to host this, "Schwarzenegger said." In a 1977 interview for OUI Magazine, published by Playboy, Arnold described to a national magazine how he and many other men all piled on one woman at Gold Gym's in Venice.

When asked whether he used drugs, Schwarzenegger replied, "Yes, grass and hash. "Schwarzenegger then went on to describe how posing for gay magazines was a great thing.

Margaret Sanger, founder of Planned Parenthood, received and gave awards to Adolf Hitler and was responsible for barbaric eugenic programs nationwide. However, its okay, they work for the New World Order.

Articles in the Associated Press, LA Weekly, and the LA Times reported that during the electricity crisis of 2001, the head of Enron, Ken Lay, met secretly with California Republicans at the Beverly Hills Hotel and pushed a plan that called for taxpayers to pay the billions in debts racked up by the states public utilities.

Schwarzenegger was part of the closed door meeting where convicted Junk-Bond felon Michael Milken and other seedy members of the establishment schemed in an attempt to keep the fraudulent deregulation going.

An Associated Press article carried in The Salt Lake City Tribune ran the headline.

"Hatch for foreign-born hopefuls."

The article continued, "Senator Orrin Hatch wants to terminate the Constitutional prohibition against foreign-born citizens such as Arnold Schwarzenegger and others from becoming president." The second Article of the Constitution states, "No person except a natural born citizen, or a citizen, or a citizen of the Unites States at the time of the adoption of this constitution, shall be eligible to the office of the president."

This can be research off the internet www.infowars.com October,2003

Congress enacted the Former Presidents Act [FPA] in 1958 to provide former Presidents an annual lifetime pension, currently $191,300, and office allowances administered by the General Services Administration [GSA.] The FPA, as amended, also provides former Presidents with travel funds and mailing privileges (3 U.S.C.102 note), also Secret Service protection for former Presidents is also authorized by statute. Proposed Legislation [P.L.] 110-161, the FY2008 Consolidated Appropriations Act, authorizes $2,478,000 in funding for former Presidents.

The President's FY2009 budget requests $2,934,000 to provide former Presidents with pensions and office allowances. Here is how it was introduce: Chief executives leaving office prior to 1958 often entered retirement pursuing various occupations and received no federal assistance. When industrialist Andrew Carnegie announced a plan in 1912 to offer $25,000 annual pensions to former Presidents, many Members of Congress deemed it inappropriate that such a pension would be provided by a private cooperation executive. That same year, legislation was first introduced to create presidential pensions. In 1955, such legislation was considered by Congress because of former President Harry S. Truman's financial limitations in hiring and office staff. Enacted in 1958, the Former Presidents Act [FPA] has been amended to provide increases in presidential pensions and the allowances for office staff.

Pensions. The Former Presidents Act, as amended, provides each former President a taxable pension that is equal to the annual rate of basic pay for the head of an executive department (Executive Level I), currently $191,300. The pension begins immediately upon a President's departure from office at noon on Inauguration Day, January 20.

The Secretary of the Treasury is responsible for making the monthly pension payments, as authorized by the Former President Act. [FPA]   A presidential widow is provided a $20,000 annual lifetime pension and ranking privileges.

The widow must waive the right to any annuity or pension under any other legislation. Mrs. Regan and Mrs. Ford do not receive the annual pensions, since they did not waive the right to any other annuity or pension provided by statue.

(Let me make it perfectly clear this information is from CRS Report RS20709, Presidential Transitions: Background and Federal Support, by Stephanie Smith.)

Transition Expenses. As authorized by the Presidential Transition Act, [PTA] as amended, transition funding is available to the outgoing Presidential and Vice President for seven months, beginning one month before the January 20 inauguration, to facilitate their relocation to private life. Based on the Department of Justice's 1974 decision, a President who resigns before his term of office has expired is also entitled to transition expenses.

In order to provide federal funding in the event of a 2004-2005 presidential transition, the President's Fiscal Year [FY2005] budget requested a total of $7.7 million. The House of Representative passed [H.R. 5025], the FY2005 Transportation, Treasury, and Independent Agencies appropriations bill, on September 22, 2004. The legislation recommended for [GSA] General Service Administration a total of $7.7 million for transition expenses.

In the Senate, [S.]2806 also recommended a total of $7.7 million to implement a possible transition. Proposed Legislation [P.L.] 108-309 was enacted on September 30, 2004, to provide continuing non-defense appropriations through November 20. A total of $2.5 million was authorized in the event of a presidential transition, until enactment of the FY2005 omnibus appropriations bill. Due to the outcome of 2004 presidential election, no funds were provided in P.L. 108-447, the FY2005 Consolidated Appropriations Act.

General Service Administration [GSA] was appropriated a total of $7.1 million for the FY2001 transition Proposed Legislation [P.L. 106-426]: $1.83 million for the outgoing Clinton Administration; $4.27 million for the incoming Bush Administration; and $1 million for General Service Administration [GSA] to provide additional assistance as required by the Presidential Transition Act of 2000.

A total of $1.5 million was appropriated for the transition expenses of outgoing President George Bush and vice President Dan Quayle [106 Stat.1729]. Of this total, the Bush Administration determined that $1.25

million would be made available to former President Bush, with the remaining $250,000 to be used by former Vice President Quayle. During his Fiscal Year [FY] 1993 transition period, former President Bush used $907,939, with an unobligated balance of $342,061. During the same period, former Vice President Quayle used $244,192 for transition expenses, with an unobligated balance of $5,808. They saw it as an opportunity to keep getting paid for doing nothing by the tax payers. Their way of seeing us as the surf's the meaning-less people.

Every government official will receive a pension for the rest of his or her life. This is granted to our Presidents, and Vice Presidents.

Remember folks they are people who volunteered to serve the people protect our interest and secure our future. Since when do you remember some one serving you come out and give you the crumbs and keep the main course?

I just have to smile at the whole situation. They are citizen before office and they return to regular citizen after office. They continue with secret service expense account. Congress has enacted this benefit into their job description so they don't have to return to work or business like a regular citizen. Who foots the bill? We the people!

Those existing President and their Vice Presidents six in all, can save us, tax payers billions of dollars that can be placed in our Social Security pension, Modern Schools with computers, lab equipment for our children' education. Build more Veterans Hospitals and clinics through out the country. We don't need more prisons. Congress manages to give themselves pay raises every two years and sometimes without our knowledge or approval. Who pays them? We the people!

For your own entertainment rent these movies; Man of the Year starring Robin Williams. Charlie Wilson's War starring Julia Roberts and Tom Hanks. These movies will reveal exclusive insight into our government.

Yet the Federal minimum wage took ten years before the people received a seventy- five cent raise to offset the cost of living. The law states that Congress is required to report what happens at the Senate, publish it or video tape. So Congress does write a very small print in the corner of the business section in USA Today or the Washington Post, or if you are late night TV watcher after Jay Lenno, and Conan O'Brien or you might see it on CSpan. We need to put a stop to this. The people we elect must come from hard working background, so they may understand the needs of the people. They have no real sense of what American steel and factory workers are going through, yet they want to replaced us, take our lively hood away, and rip us off. They're taking our clothing manufactures' and automobile factories to cheap labor countries to shatter the economy of our country. Then sell to you the American consumer at a higher profit. That's how the rich are able to say isn't America great. We are suckers. USA! As we continue on this path our children's future will be bleak. <u>WAKE UP AMERICA!</u>

We are a bright and colorful country as we should be. Set apart from any other country, or nations. We the people in the early thirty, forty's through fifty's were trendsetters. The U.S. is a sprinkle of many races and culture. Now America has blended into the tail instead of being the Head. Great example; the Electric Car EV1 was introduce by General Motors April 24th 2003 these cars were leased to residents and then they were told that they have to give up the cars or face disciplinary action, by the beginning of March 15, 2005.

GIVE US OUR ELECTRIC CAR!

General Motors revealed several prototype variants of the EV1 drive-train at the 1998 <u>Detroit Auto Show</u>. United States Government "The Feds" sued California for developing a mandate for alternative fuel and then told them they must give it up take the cars off the roads. More details of "Who Killed the Electric Car" by Filmmaker Chris Paine, download and watch it.

The next market of the future is The SKY Car. Designer and Inventor is UC Davis Professor Paul Moller. We can see him as the Henry Ford and Wright Brothers of the future urbanite.

He's developed the car for everyday use to commute to and from work, malls, supermarkets,

Emergency rescue, Police protection and be able to park in normal parking spaces in your own garage. I like this! I want one!

GIVE US OUR SKYCAR!

Go to his web-site <u>www.moller.com</u> General Motors and Oil Companies don't want him to market his Sky-Car because he also offer an alternative fuel for his vehicles. OOOH---RAHHH! **SEMPER-FIDELIS** means: [always faithful]

Our Government once more is waiting for another country like Japan, or China to bring it forth, then get on the Johnnie come lately wagon.

Mr. Moller has developed the Sky-Car and improving it for more than 30 years. The Federal Government is not willing to leave it in the hands of a civilian. As usual they (F.G.) want a Big piece of the pie for something they had no contribution.

Nations has drawn from our strengths, taken, and not given any thing back, no loans paid back to which our last three Presidents in the span of twenty-four years has disappointed and let down the people of the United States. <u>WAKE UP AMERICA!</u>

We know what politicians do! If politicians were running our company, we as the Board of trusties we would fire them. Our Country is formed to develop our Republic and Democratic way of life, and not to be push around by other Nations telling us what to do, and how to govern ourselves. We began our Nation under Godly laws and Biblical principals in which we were doing a great job. Two hundred and seventy five years later we are changing what we set out to do, for a few individuals who think we should ratify the Constitution to suit their needs. Some politicians who are currently in office feel they should change the Constitution to accommodate <u>one</u> not the <u>majority of the</u> <u>People.</u> It works let's not change anything. Your fore-fathers did not form this Union of our Republic and Democratic Society way of life to force others to our way of life.

Those immigrants who lived in other countries saw the United States as a place for freedom without any restrictions. I can get use to this way of life. Don't! get it into your head that since you have planted some roots you can change the rules to make it better. Forget about it.! Just leave as you came, or shed some blood for this flag and country and enjoy the fruits of our labor. Godfathering or (Invading) other Countries expecting them to conform to our ideals, it's why we left the British Colonies.

When we are asked to help our neighboring Countries, then and only then we should assess the situation. We don't always have to be Big Brother or change their way of life. We must respect their culture understand their rights. We may then have a better perspective on how we are to proceed. We should show respect, and only then, we will be respected. Other Countries would not threaten our way of life by attacking our soil. Have we learned that it is not so pretty when you see what we love is being rip-apart, and destroyed?

The news media showed the horrific destruction of the Twin Towers over and over so they were working on getting people to re-live the horror and pain to gain ratings. Not concerning them-selves on what those who suffered loss were going through.

It was our second time a country or terrorist brought destruction to our shores. To which our President had to declare War.

America could not believe it was happening to us again. We are a super powerful Nation. People thought it was the end. We are still suffering from the effects of how we travel from city to city country to country. Terrorists wanted to stop our way of life confuse and disrupt our freedoms. They succeeded at that, we are prisoners at our airports. We can't travel with the assurance of safety, worrying constantly about the comforts of small items that we took for granted. <u>WAKE UP AMERICA</u>!

Don't continue to allow the open door policy to foreigners, with out work permits, legal visa and enforce them to leave at the end of their stay then resubmit papers. Our Commander in Chief did not step up to the challenge. Instead he formed a new federal agency [HLS] Home Land Security to place himself in history. That caused taxpayers more money. He should be removed from his post. Let him pick up the tab. Put an experienced Warrior in charge. President Bush is still guessing. I don't mean an old [warrior] man with remembrance of the old days.

We the people should not allow just anyone to tear away the fiber of our Red White and Blue or give them a notion of what it's like to be an American. Every American male, female should serve the minimum of four years in the Armed Forces.

At this time in our congressional history we do not have representatives in office that has spent any time in the military active duty. This is to exclude our X-Presidents' Carter, Bush, V.P. Mondale, and Late Honorable President John F. Kennedy. To know what it is like to be fired upon or to engage in live fire in order to protect our liberties, "to do to go," our freedom, our flag and our way of life. " OOOH- RAHH!!!" <u>WE THE PEOPLE</u> should only allow eight years minimum for elected officials in office. The people and not the

President of USA should appoint Supreme Courts Justices. These Justices office should only be active for fifteen years. The President should only hold office for one term and only with the success of accomplishing 75-85% of what he/she set out to do to qualify for a second term. Allowing them continue secret service protection for the first two years for acclamation and no expense account, or expense account to his family after death. They are regular citizens and no longer should the American taxpayers support them. We the people should not be responsible for five living X-Presidents and Vice Presidents expenses. We have it on record that most of our great leaders or Presidents were men of military background. President George Washington. Our Twenty Century President Teddy Roosevelt, who formed his own Rough Riders to fight for our freedom and began the building of the Panama Canal. General and President Dwight Eisenhower, General McArthur, General Patton, General Schwarzkopf, President J.F. Kennedy he was a Naval Officer and now General Colin Powell.

They were and are men of vision. These men all understood what the plight of our Country entailed. There's was a structure of dignity and love of every American, and what it means to carry on the Tradition of our fore Fathers and this Great Nation.

President Jimmy Cater was on the right track. He had vision. He made strong statements that we will no longer buy oil outside the United States, it upset the Texans, he took steps to clean air and renew energy by being the first to place Solar- Panels on the White House. He had a military background and he was a doer and still is. This writer would take a bullet for him. After Nixon all the following Presidents have disgraced our country and tainted the flag. There main concern was to muck things up and build a library in their honor. Why would anyone pay to see what someone did in screwing things up, skipping around the truth. If you did the job expected of you, compatriots would erect a library in your honor. You shouldn't have to build a library. It tells us that you are looking for pat on your back, an atta-boy. The Politician's of today are only looking at monetary worth and placing their names in history, not the pursuit of equality, long Gevity, security and the pursuit of every living soul having the opportunity to succeed in their desire of true happiness. Politicians' constant thought is how can we get richer and keep the people they represent down trodden and poor.

Elected officials should represent the will of the American people. That is why we vote them into office, for what they say, promise, and give strong stance too.

Governors in each state should consider a pardon for men and women who have reformed their lives. Allowing them to regain some liberty, they once knew. Help them back into the work force. We seem to build more prisons and who is footing the bill? We the people! We should be rebuilding lives, not more prisons. People in prison would love to be a part of society again. If given the task to bear arms to fight and protect this country they would see it as an opportunity to share with their family, friends what they can contribute.

There are so many people in prison that they have fallen through the cracks of justice. Allow those who have served and changed the opportunity to join the military. These men and women would pull together once they knew that while they were incarcerated they could not be included in what our Nation is fighting to protect.

When given the chance everyone would like to know that he or she did something positive even if it means to give his/her life to a worthy cause such as protecting the freedom of his/her families and this country. We can mess with our own country but no other foreign country can! The prison system is and always has been a big money business. Governors, District Attorneys and Sheriff make their budget by locking up citizens.

This office was and still is a voluntary post, should not include all the extra benefits and salary hype they give themselves. All Congresspersons and Senators should only hold office for eight years. These elected government officials should be taxed 45% of their income and not to include expense accounts. We the people did not ask them to apply for those jobs they decide to run for office. They should only consider a pay increase with the understanding that the rest of the Nation is receiving a minimum pay raise so to the high cost of living. Let them understand the burden that citizens contented.

We need to stop voting men or women into government office who are un-ethical, have not made sacrifices and who have been involved in criminal acts. Some of these are Pres. Nixon was caught with his hand in the cookie jar. Pres. Ford pardon, Pres. Nixon. Allowing Pres. Clinton who was a draft dodger and as a Governor he and his wife Hillary have poisoned so many people lives.

Bill Clinton gave up our shipping ports to foreign countries. He gave up our automobile factories, to other countries so he and the GM industry, would profit from taking money out of the pockets of American people and diminishing their lives.

Hillary Clinton decided to run for Senator of New York, when she never lived or held any office in New York. Three weeks after John F. Kennedy Jr. voiced his opinion quote Clintons are not New Yorkers. They should go back where they came. He and his wife, unborn baby and sister –in-law was faced with a fatal accident. It was excused as inexperience pilot and bad weather, with no other explanation or further investigation of their death. Hillary Clintons would not have made a bump in the run for Senator in New York with John Jr. running.

As it has been expressed by the media Sen. McCain is contradicting his early attempt to becoming a chameleonic in saying what he feels the public wants to hear. He is not doing the job he was elected in office as Senator for Arizona. It's one of the largest military retired communities in America. There are seniors who are not claiming to be spouse any more, so they can receive Social Security benefits as individuals. So they can survive in an accelerating economy. They must file taxes as individuals. Our government would penalize them when they file jointly. These are Americans who both have worked all there lives, raised their children, and would like to receive their fair share of the Social Security System they paid into, without jeopardizing their medical care and prescription needs. Most seniors 65-72 are force to continue working at small jobs so they can afford food, and medication for survival. Whenever, I go into or around supermarkets, my eyes tear-up… for I see those who forged and paid their dues are subject to continued slaving.

They are all honest law-biding citizen who have fought or lost love ones in wars. It's time we the People put a stop to this. WE are tired of the BANKERS, LAWYERS and POLITICIANS. They must pay as those who steal, rob, or murder. They should be jailed without pardon, or excused on good behavior. They must be made to pay back all they stole or flog on National T.V. They are killing families. We should mandate severe consequences. As those, we put to the three-strike law. It has been going on for more than five decades that men and women are incarcerated for lack of proper defense, evidence, and finance. Yet we see so many people who are guilty and some times admit guilt however, they can afford legal ridiculous defense they often repeat the same crime again.

We were once a Nation that other countries wanted to be. Instead of staying focus and on track, we began looking at what other countries were doing. The Europeans they have an open accede to invite sex and nudity at public beaches.

We have adapted to popularizing sex, nudity and violence on TV, movies and video games.

City Civil Servants

We the people should now consider the working civil servant such as Police Officers, Sheriff they should not be tax during their rookie and up to the level of Sergeant in the field. Once they received Officer rank or no longer working in the streets. They will have a tax responsibility of 10% of their income. If they have secondary employment in the same field, they should not pay additional taxes. If the job were in a different field, they would have to earn more than their primary job to pay additional taxes. The Police officers should respect the people they promise to protect, more than they do and they would receive respect. Too many young and seasoned veterans are quick to pull their gun to shoot and kill at the little infraction of any threat to them. Yet they attend an eight to ten week academy to learn the law and subdue a suspect.

We have seen on the news media and local shows how strong and able officers grab women and drag them out of their vehicle. So often they answer domestic calls and end up causing one or both injuries. Everything should be tried before using deadly force. Or officers shouldn't be on the job. Citizens should feel comfortable and not worry when a police approach them. Instead they begin to get scared, nervous and hope they are not- probing to see if you fall into the possibility of guilty. You can kiss it good-bye if you are white with Tattoos, look like American Indian or East Indian, Japanese, black man young with loud music or well dressed in the upper class neighborhood. Officers find themselves saying in their patrol car, I can't wait to bust that dirt bag. How I know? I have been on plenty of ride along. That's when you observe the accounts of a full day on the job with an officer and his/her partner.

These men and women should be paid hazardous pay, their job is very stressful and demanding, so they would treat the public with more respect.

Until the tragic of 911, Firefighters were not considered heroes until the world saw how so many sacrificed themselves to save others.

Our Firefighters and Paramedics are men and women who put their lives on the line for us the citizens of our neighborhoods and communities.

They give up many special hours away from their families to do a job that not everyone is really capable and dedicated to do, with out any concern for themselves, yet keeping safety first. This would give the opportunity for these brave souls to be able to sustain life at a comfortable level without struggles. This will also help keep people to be more honest and looking out for their neighbors. Our educators, such-as teachers, not be taxed unless they reached the pay level of over 120,000 a year.

Why are we allowing the teachers who are to train our children to be paid peanuts they should begin at a minimum of $80,000 and given outstanding medical benefits for their family? Given all the updated resources to complete their jobs they so love. They are special and we entrust them with our children [precious jewels]. Why are we not supporting them in full access to discipline our hard headed and un-attentive un-read video-minded children?

This would encourage teachers to continue to evolve to greatness for our kids. The Board of education is spending more time to separate our teachers from the students with detectors than finding solutions to pulling them together. Set proper dress policy so children are not having indecent apparels. Parents should support the school. This should be part of school dress code.

Famous Fabulous and
Their Off-springs

We the people should regard certain professional athletics, entertainers and Executives, CEO and Presidents of major companies should be responsible in rebuilding the deprived areas in their community.

These well to do Professional Athletics, millionaires, and billionaires should be burden the blunt of taxes for if it was not for the everyday working class buying their tickets or products they wouldn't be where they are. That is at least 25% of their gross without tax cuts, unless they were to donate such as Hospitals, Condos, Homes, Schools and Vocational Colleges, Recreational Center offering people in the community the training for them to work from their own areas. This would help to keep the kids active and adults employed and off the streets. Not claiming that it's not being done. We need lots more donations.

We should bring back the draft system or make it mandatory for all to serve in the military for the minimum of four years. If he or she desires to run for any political office, they would be required to serve eight years in active duty capacity. This will ensure that they shall have full experience in sacrifices and dedication to what protection of our freedom is all about. When it comes time to defend our shores or our Air space they would not be so eager to send our children off to conflicts or war.

Every major city in the <u>STATES</u> should freeze on buying gas, for three days out mainly on the weekends. This Government is trying to have us adapt life the Japanese. Their plan is to keep raising the gas prices so we have to go mass transportation and depend on the government. We are a society of free people. If we do not fight now give up some of our comforts we will loose it all.

Stop the ticket purchase of all the professional sports for three months. Let us have all the different Arenas empty. The athletics will not be able to get their large salaries that we provide for them.

These are people that go around playing games while we sit in the stands eating peanuts, crackerjacks, popcorn, hot dogs and drinking beer. While they are eating, prime ribs, steak, caviar and drinking Champagne. Professional Athletes in the days of Mickey Mantle, Roger Maris, Roberto Clemente, Hank Aaron, Dr. J, Bill Walton, to name a few. They weren't receiving the bloated salary. Fathers were able to afford to see these professionals without loosing their lunch for the next three weeks. I do like to visit or attend a game to root for my favorite team. I was never able to afford to take my entire family to a pro game of any type. Owners would have to tighten their belts, realize that in order to provide opportunity for all walks of people to fill the stands.

Many others such as your fathers mothers and grand parents did not come to AMERICA with their hope and dreams to give their children the opportunity for a better life to have us, the BABY BOOMERS to give it away without any sacrifice. Generation X is having it easy for so many are just having everything handed over to them without them really earning or sacrificing for what they want.

There are parents bribing their children with a car if they keep their grades up or graduate. The nation has a head count of 16,000 deaths of teens drinking and driving, according to ALL STATE statistics. They are not mature to have keys placed in their hands for themselves and placing other lives in danger.

It should be mandatory for parents to refuse them the privilege to drive until they are twenty years of age. The extra four-year wait would cut the death toll in half. There was a family who bought their daughter a small compact and she took a joy ride with two other friends. She lost control of her car and did not have her seat belt on. They lost their daughter and were not able to see her receive her diploma. She had a very promising future she was the first to be accepted to College in her family.

The Book of ISAIAH 1: 4, 7, 9-10 (The New International Version) We are a sinful Nation of people loaded with guilt a brood of evildoers, children given to corruption! They have forsaken the LORD; the only Holy One of Israel without sin and turned their backs on him.

Verse: 7

Your country is desolate, your cities burned with fire; your fields are being stripped by foreigners right before you, laid waste as when overthrown by strangers.

Verse: 9

Unless the LORD Almighty had left us some survivors, we would become like Sodom, we would have been like Gomorrah.

Verse: 10

Hear the word of the LORD, you rulers of Sodom;
Listen to the law of GOD, You people of Gomorrah!

Some of the mighty men and women that are committed to teaching God's Word for its people sake are;

Billy Graham   Dr. Frederick K.C. Price, Dr. Creflo & Taffi Dollar, Dr. Tom & Maureen Anderson, Kenneth & Gloria Copeland, Bishop T.D.Jakes, Bishop Charles Blake Jesse & Cathy Duplantis, Pastor Marcellus and Shunta Dukes of Solid Foundation Bible Church,   Joyce Meyers, Pastor Joel Olsten, Oral J. Roberts, Pat Roberts, Paul Crouch, and John Hagee, are amongst the many.

We have allowed the National Anthem removed out of public, private schools. Prayers banned. The minority are controlling what the Constitution expressed for the majority to be a Godly Nation. We are found under those principals. There are so many video games being develop with so much blood and violence that kids don't realize that in real life you don't get back up.

Dr. Julia Hare Director of Black Ink Tank, and Author: Miss Education of Black Children. Express : "Our Child Care system put the fear in parents by subjecting them to be arrested for physical discipline[spanking]". This was the first step for the government taking control. Second, allowing the school teacher to place our boys and girls in detention. Keeping them from regular classes was preparing them for incarceration. Once imprisoned and released. They get a parole officer who gets paid to make it impossible to fit in society. They are not given the opportunity to get an above minimum wage job, because they must report that they are a felon. If they were to slip through the cracks get ahead with a great job.

They later learn that he or she has to pay taxes and cannot vote, or own property. Now we have a great system that shows how we have citizens without taxation and legal representation. Where are those people Constitutional Rights?

The parents are afraid of the social system, the teachers are afraid of the Principal the Principals are afraid of the School Boards and the School Boards are afraid of the State and the children are not afraid of anyone. Our society gives them time out, instead of a firm hand. We are now faced with children as young as sixth graders killing students, teachers and parents. The kids are not afraid of anyone because we don't discipline them.

It started with the Menendez Brothers killing their parents in August, of 1989. The nation was shocked. This then led to TV Movie and allowing the Media to pump it up. Then Colleges and its now reached Elementary Schools. These are the same people we say have served their time and should be given a new start. It doesn't happen for all walks of races.

I awake every morning crying that all that I sacrificed was for nothing. As a veteran of Viet Nam there's not a day I say why are we not taking care of each other, the wounded and sick military. We should not have any military family in the states living with lack of shelter, food, medical and general care for their fighting military. Our government is taxing active duty military while in active status. These men and women who are doing the job our elected officials are not willing to do or capable of doing.

They as I would give their lives at the drop of a hat defending their post, liberty, and their unborn and born children for the RED WHITE and BLUE that flows over every Americans Home, Business, School, Government Building. Let's not repeat History as what Tavis Smiley the Author of The Covenant and Founder of STATE OF THE BLACK UNION. His many guest:

Dr. Cornel West stated that America was once cooperation before it became Union. U.S. was just out to make a profit. We are reverting to our old ways. My proposal to change in the right direction to fire, resign, clean house of all the Senate, Congressmen who has been in office capacity for more than fifteen years. Who haven't brought any positive law proposal to the house?

We need fresh and productive ideas so we can continue to grow. While in Viet-Nam my voting privilege was not a question nor was my death for eighteen year old.

Each Administration changes their approach, never direction. We have had the Clintons, Bushes and now more promises that they need more time to change. Each political leader had two terms to do something. We keep hearing we are on the verge "of choking our selves".

We the hardworking citizens need to know there more for our future than just promises. We will always encounter immigrants. Our nation is made up of immigrants. We had a surge of Italians that brought us to our knees for a depression. Then we had Asians after WWII.

The end of the Viet Nam war, we had a surge of Vietnamese where our California ports were over run to where Marine Corps Base Camp Pendleton set up Tent Camps to house the immigrants. As you know then came the Cubans. Our country has not placed fast and firm policy on making sure if you are not properly set with a visa, sponsor and permit to work with a specific employer and job. You will be refused passage to our country. We are now approaching a new era. This author has served voluntary in the military for twenty-one years for six presidents and they made some success and others that were just going through the motions. WAKE UP AMERICA

Have you put our nation to a query where are we? I am in my late fifties and become more troubled that as a man, my fellow man who walks the same streets as I have not taken the same interest in what it means to give up his freedom and career for a short time to pay his dues. In helping to protect the safety, right of speech, freedom to be, do, go anywhere, to worship, and hold true to the meaning of FREEDOM.

The British left England so they could form a New Government that gave all men a chance to live as equals. Those Founding Fore-Fathers had the right idea, but they were Caucasian and they kept it far too long without a change or a mix up of people of color to add to their flavor. They had the right idea by using Godly principals of what our Country should be lead by, respecting other Nations and culture of people. That's why they left England and formed a new World.

I have witnessed so many politicians and soccer mom who are throwing in their own personal beliefs and confusing the political process. Others before them has made sacrifices in giving up their own riches or freedom and as dear as their lives. So that others and their children can know what freedom is truly about!

Information is from: The WALLBUILDER REPORT

We had a group of Black Politicians who were the First Blacks in Congress to serve they were:

> Hiram Revels, Benjamin Turner, Robert C. DeLarge, Josiah T. Walls, Jefferson H. Long, Joseph H. Rainey and Robert Brown Elliot.

American democracy was only decades old rather than centuries ago. Until the 1965 Voting Rights Act when blacks could vote did democracy truly begin.

Such a declaration does not accurately portray the history of black voting in America nor does it honor the thousands of blacks who sacrificed their lives obtaining the right to vote and who exercised that right as long as two centuries ago. I just can't state that fact enough. We today are completely unaware that it was not Democrats but was actually Republicans , like the seven men pictured on the cover, who not only helped achieve the passage of explicit constitutional voting rights for blacks in 1870 but who also held hundreds of elected offices during the 1800s.

Black Voting in the 1870s

The infamous 1856 *Dred Scott* decision in which a Democratic controlled US Supreme Court observed that "blacks had no rights which a white man was bound to respect; and that the Negro might justly and lawfully be reduced to slavery for his benefit." Non-Democrat Justice Benjamin R. Curtis, one of only two on the Court who dissented in that opinion, provided a lengthy documentary history to show that many blacks in America had often exercised the rights of citizens

That many at the time of the American Revolution "possessed the franchise of [voters] on equal terms with other citizens" State constitutions protecting voting rights for blacks included those of Delaware (1776), Maryland (1776), New Hampshire (1784), and New York (1777), (Constitution signer

Rufus King declare that in New York, "a citizen of color was entitled to all the privileges of a citizen [and] entitled to vote.")

Pennsylvania also extended such rights in her 1776 constitution, as did Massachusetts in her 1780 constitution. In fact, nearly a century later in 1874, US Rep. Robert Brown Elliott (a black Republican from SC) queried:

"When did Massachusetts sully her proud record by placing on her statute, book any law which admitted to the ballot the white man and shut out the black man? She has never done it; she will not do it."

As a result of these provisions, early American towns such as Baltimore had more blacks than whites voting in elections; and when the proposed US Constitution was placed before citizens in 1787 and 1788, it was ratified by both black and white voters in a number of States.

This is not to say that we haven't come a long way, we just need to be reminded that since the Republicans and all the white [Caucasians] has sold our country out to foreigners in Auto manufacturing and textiles and electronics to save on labor cost. Those, major cooperation's are taking away earnings and livelihood from the American citizens. Great example is General Motors in the city of Detroit one of the major American Car Manufacture is practically a ghost town. We as a people of color should consider how important it is to join in the political process to registering for the party of choice and voting come November.

There came a time when our parents and grand parents would say, those who are first will be last and those who are last will be first. History had it at one time in the early 1700-1800s'.

Although Great Britain had prohibited the abolition of slavery in the Colonies before the Revolution, as Independent States they were free to end slavery – as occurred in Pennsylvania, Massachusetts, Connecticut, Rhode Island, Vermont, New Hampshire, and New York.

Additionally, blacks in many early States not only had the right to vote but also the right to hold office. Elias Boudinot, who helped frame the Bill of Rights, was one of the many Founding Fathers who opposed pro-slavery policies such as the Missouri Compromise. This permitted the admission of new slave- holding States. This policy was loudly lamented and strenuously opposed by the few Founders remaining alive. I mention this in my book because there were so many black men who help forge the Democratic and Republican fabric of our way of life today. Fifty African Americans were elected as Republicans to the South Carolina legislature after the Civil War. Also in Texas, forty two blacks were elected to the State Legislature, 127 to Louisiana's, 99 to Alabama's Legislature.

These Republicans took the steps to turn and move quickly to protect voting rights for blacks, prohibit segregation, formed public education, and public transportation, State police, juries, and other institutions to blacks. With all this we have contributed it's not shown in the U.S. history. Those men have paved the way we in-turn will accept the baton. We as a race and a people have accepted for years the leadership of White and respected the office of the President and never questioned it.

Now after 35 President and 100 years it's now time to have a little color and change of view, there is worry and speculations that this man is not going to be looking out for the good of the general public.

Senator Barack Obama is what the working American is all about. I wouldn't call him average, but I do see him as one that we as citizens can say we can hope for a new. With his wife Michelle Obama as First Lady we can identify with hopes and dreams of new America.

We were considered to be a race of people who could not think reason or read. Yet with all the accomplishments and contribution to this Country and we are hardly mentioned in History books. If not by force of determination we are always proving ourselves to be a race of first and not last as some would like for us to think.

With the marvel of the internet, more people should take more time to …search… who successfully perfected blood plasma, traffic light, many use of peanut, heart transplant and hundred others.

National Geographic has always showed pictures of Native Africans in their natural attire and culture, with so many piercing of all types to where the White America would say as if it was unusual and awful. It was considered barbaric, although it is our culture. We were kidnapped from our native

African soil. Native American had their soil taken and was also consider savages.

We were continuing a culture of our race or tribe. This was considered so in the early sixties.

Now you see so many copy cats young and mid-age adults who are faking or imitating similar features who don't know why it's done or the meaning of the culture. In all respect it is disrespectful and a mockery. Today a race of people who sit in the sun to gain a tan, braid their hair, walk with a swag gel, imitate our dance sound of music speech has the nerve to call us monkeys. Who are the ones mimicking to have an identity? We should all work as a team and look for ways to see everyday as Christmas, Thanksgiving, or Olympics.

I believe I have seen it all. I recall approaching a newly opened shopping center early one Saturday morning searching for a store, a woman stepped in front of my vehicle, not seeing her I stopped and proceeded to roll down my window. I offered my apology for not seeing them. This mother of probably 32 years old was with her son of possible fourteen years old had sadly given me the finger and then called me a nigger. This is a lesson that when her son is in school he would wonder when he says this word, why was he suspended out of school. He gets into a fight what's wrong? Before I knew it I had called her a witch, which showed my lack of control and made me ashamed of action. This young teenager witness what a parent should not do in-front of their child. That's how hatred begins, out of the mother's mouth to child's ear. This is 2008 and we still live like this? How sad.

<u>Wake Up America</u>*!*

Resources

Democracy Now (2008) Suicide or Murder? Three years after the death of Pfc.LaVena Johnson in Iraq, her parents continue their call for investigation, July 23, 2008, Retrieved August 18, 2008 from

http://www.democracynow.org/2008/7/23/suicide_or_murder_three_years_ after

White, Josh (2005) Washington Post, May 23, 2005; pA01, Tillman's parents are critical of army, Retrieved September 17, 2008, from

www.washingtonpost.com

If you wonder, then I provoke thought.

Let's WAKE UP AMERICA!
GOD BLESS AMERICA.
WE THE PEOPLE

I dedicate this book to US Marines, Army, Air Force, Navy, National Guard those before after and those families who suffered a lost love one.

By GySgt Maximo D Cordoba USMC Ret.

www.ingramcontent.com/pod-product-compliance
Lightning Source LLC
Chambersburg PA
CBHW060646290526
45793CB00001B/422

*9 7 8 1 4 4 0 1 0 3 6 0 5 *